Guide to Fitness

Guide to Fitness

A comprehensive guide to fitness with simple exercises

Bath · New York · Singapore · Hong Kong · Cologne · Delhi
Melbourne · Amsterdam · Johannesburg · Auckland · Shenzhen

Caution

Please check with your doctor/therapist before attempting these workouts, particularly if you are suffering from an injury, are pregnant, or have just had a baby. It is recommended that new mothers wait at least six weeks postpartum before participating in exercise (12 weeks if it was a Caesarean birth). If you feel any pain or discomfort at any time, please stop exercising immediately and seek medical advice.

First published by Parragon in 2012

Parragon
Queen Street House
4 Queen Street
Bath, BA1 1HE
www.parragon.com

See page 144 for photograph copyright details
Text © Parragon Books Ltd 2012

Produced by Guy Croton

ISBN 978-1-4454-6988-1

Printed in China

Contents

Starting out

The following pages will help you understand how your body works, and explain how you can improve your health and fitness. There's information on what you need to do before you start, including safety tips, fitness options, and creating the right environment, so you can exercise safely. Plus, you'll find out how to improve your posture, a crucial part of any fitness plan.

Introduction

If you want to start on the road to getting fit without spending hours in the gym, this is the book for you. The old saying "no pain, no gain," is often true, but the exercises aren't meant to be a daily chore; instead, you should enjoy each day and look forward to trying new experiences.

The best way to get and keep fit is to have a daily routine of regular exercises, which combine all the muscle groups. This will bring you noticeable benefits, help you achieve a healthier life, and make you feel good as well.

While this fitness regime will bring you and your body many benefits, those benefits can be greatly increased if you are aware that what goes into your body and how you treat it also affects your fitness. Also, a fit body needs a fit mind because when you are doing daily exercises you will require determination and motivation.

This book covers a wide range of information that explains how to achieve a healthy lifestyle, and contains all the exercises (with instructions and a 12-week plan) that you will need to make a real difference to your overall fitness level and general well-being.

As well as targeting all the body zones, the stretching and core stability exercises offer a practical range of beneficial routines. So even if your fitness goals change, this book will still be useful. You

Exercise can:

- Tone and strengthen muscles.
- Improve your overall physical and mental well-being.
- Help prevent heart disease, strokes, and diabetes (Type 2).
- Reduce high blood cholesterol and high blood pressure.
- Prevent arthritis setting in, help improve bad circulation, and guard against osteoporosis.
- Relieve general stress and anxiety-related problems as well as improving sleep problems.

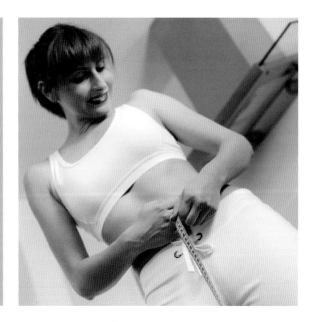

don't need any expensive equipment for the majority of the exercises, and can choose to buy an exercise ball for the core stability routines if you wish.

All the exercises have been tried and tested by experts in the field and have been found to be very effective. They really do work, so let's get started!

Great reasons for getting fitter

Apart from the obvious benefit of improving your overall health and appearance, taking time to exercise and care for your body will really pay dividends in many other ways. Strengthening your muscles will improve your balance and posture, and increase your flexibility, helping to keep your body in tiptop condition as you get older. As an added bonus, you'll find it easier to control your weight, because muscles burn more calories than fat.

Exercise is also known to boost levels of "happy hormones" (endorphins) in the brain, making you feel more cheerful and relaxed, with a higher sense of self-esteem. Endorphins also beat stress, so you'll not only be a dream to work with, but you're also more likely to perform to your best abilities. And when you're feeling optimistic, you're more likely to make healthy food choices, which will further help you to achieve your goals.

The way to **fitness**

No more excuses about starting tomorrow or next week, there's no time like today. Once you have decided to undertake a fitness program, rest assured that you will not regret it, so start planning now and let's work toward your dream of achieving a leaner and fitter body!

The exercises in this book are all easy to follow. If practiced correctly and regularly, they will help improve your physical and mental well-being and strengthen muscle tone, without it costing too much or having to spend hours working out in the gym.

All-round fitness

By following the exercise plans featured later on (*see* page 126) you will greatly improve your fitness levels, but if you really want to get fit then you'll need to make sure your diet is healthy, too.

Tips for good practice

Exercising alone means that you don't have a teacher to help ensure that you practice carefully and so you will need to take full responsibility for your own safety. Make sure you:

- Always do both warm-up and cool-down exercises for at least five minutes to make sure that your heart rate changes slowly and you don't hurt any muscles.
- Never "work through the pain" when exercising; you will only hurt yourself.

- Drink plenty of water during and after your workout to prevent dehydration and muscle stiffness.
- Don't rush the moves—analyze what you're doing: it's about quality, not just quantity.
- Wear appropriate clothing that allows you to move freely and comfortably. Avoid becoming constricted.
- Follow an exercise program that meets your needs, but make sure that your needs and goals are realistic.

Starting off

If you're a beginner, you may want to ease yourself gently into the exercise plan and do fewer repetitions. That's fine—just remember to be persistent and your efforts will pay off. Soon enough, you'll find that your body will be better able to cope with the routine and, when this happens, you'll know you've made amazing progress.

The neutral position

For some of the exercises you will be asked to keep your spine in neutral. This means making sure your spine is in the right position when you are exercising, which will help you get much better results.

Standing in Neutral Spine

Stand with your feet hip-width apart and turn your toes slightly outward. Make sure that your body weight is evenly distributed between the feet, as well as between the front and back regions of the foot. Roll the foot inward and outward to find the point where the weight of the body is centered. Keep the head straight and level. Try to keep the spine straight but do not overarch the back. The shoulders should be straight and level with the floor.

Lying on your back in Neutral Spine

Lie on your back with your knees bent and feet on the floor, hip-width apart. The ankles, knees, and hips should be aligned. The knees should be stable, and the lower back touching the floor should feel the weight of the body. The shoulders and back of your ribs should be touching the floor and you should feel the weight of your upper body on them. The center of the back should naturally lift off the floor. The neck should be lengthened away from the body.

The following points should be kept in mind during Neutral Position:

- The ankles, hips, and shoulders should be aligned.
- Each side of the body should carry equal weight.
- The muscles should be relaxed.

Warming **up**

The warm-up exercises will help you release any tension held in the mind or body before you start on your exercise session. They will also mobilize and stretch all the muscles in preparation for the more demanding exercises. It is essential to do these warm-ups, whichever exercises you then choose to move on to.

Loosening up the body before exercising is important because it prepares the muscles and joints for the workout and also increases the heart rate. Consequently, the harder the muscles work, the more beneficial the exercise will be. Warm-up exercises should be a blend of rhythmic stretching so that all parts of the body are limbered up and ready to go.

Each of the five exercise chapters begins with a series of warm-up exercises. The idea is that you choose a couple of the exercises shown and allow the time to warm up thoroughly.

Starting gently

If you are completely new to exercising, you can limit your session to the warm-up exercises only, just for a week or two, so you can really ease into the exercise routine. It is also a good idea to stick to the warm-up movements only for a short while, if you have not taken any form of exercise for some time and perhaps feel stiff and inflexible as a result. You may find that this stage is enough of a challenge in itself at first, but in no time at all you will have loosened up your joints and started to improve your muscle tone, and you will feel ready, able, and keen to tackle the next step.

Cooling **down**

Many people dismiss cooling down after exercise as a waste of time or simply unimportant. In reality, the cool-down is just as important as the warm-up if you want to stay injury free. However, while the main purpose of warming up is to prepare the body and mind for exercising, cooling down and stretching play different roles.

The main aim of the cool-down is to promote recovery and return the body to a pre-exercise level and, as long as it is performed properly, to assist your body in its necessary repair process. As with the warm-ups, each of the five chapters features a series of cool-down exercises. Again, the idea is that you choose a couple of the exercises shown and allow around ten minutes to stretch and cool down.

The cool-down will also help with "post-exercise muscle soreness." It does this by allowing the muscles to repair and align themselves after the exercises. This prevents the soreness that is usually experienced the day after a workout, particularly if you haven't done any exercise for a while.

Cooling down and stretching also increase your flexibility, which means you will be able to have a fuller range of movement through your joints.

While most forms of exercise will help you to burn calories and fat while strengthening and defining the muscles, stretching helps to tone and lengthen them. The result is that you can appear slimmer, even if you haven't lost any weight.

Effective **exercising**

You might be wondering whether a short exercise session each day is enough to make a difference to your body, but the good news is that it works. The most effective way to burn off excess fat is to work the body aerobically, and we show you how!

We recommend that you start with our plan and monitor your results, but only you will know your body's major trouble zones, so you can include extra exercises to target those particular areas. Once you become familiar with the exercises, you can easily draw up your own plan.

Easy steps

This book divides the main body zones into four chapters, each of which targets a specific trouble area. The sections contain warm-ups, exercises, and cool-down stretches, and are thoroughly explained later in the book. The exercises are divided into two levels—introductory and advanced —so that you can start your program off at an easy pace and increase the number of repetitions as you progress.

These sections are followed by a chapter explaining the benefits of core stability, which includes suggestions and exercises to help you train your core muscles.

The final chapter contains a 12-week exercise planner that will allow you to work at your own pace and, ultimately, achieve your fitness goals.

The planner is organized into two sections—introductory and advanced. Once you've worked through the introductory, or first six-week schedule, and are feeling more confident and fitter, you can progress to the second series of exercises. The plans can be used as an outline guide, so if you find any particular exercises difficult, you can replace them with something else from the same level.

Warming up

Targets: To prepare your muscles for exercise.

What's involved: A range of gentle body movements to prepare the body for more strenuous exercises.

Benefits: Warm up to avoid injuries.

Exercises

Targets: Each of the major muscle groups in the body.

What's involved: A wide variety of exercises that are fun to do.

Benefits: An all-over improvement in muscle tone and shape.

Cooling down and stretching

Targets: To cool down after an exercise session and to help prevent muscle soreness.

What's involved: A series of stretches that will leave your mind calm and your body more flexible.

Benefits: To help cool your body down, while making your muscles longer, leaner, and more toned.

Exercise plans

Targets: All-over body fitness and toning.

What's involved: A series of exercises that progress through a 12-week plan.

Benefits: The way to fitness for those new to exercise.

Core stability

Targets: A workout that strengthens your body from the inside out.

What's involved: A series of exercises that will strengthen your core.

Benefits: Your balance and coordination will be improved.

Standing **posture**

Posture is the starting point of all movement. If your posture is under strain, every movement you make will be inefficient, which leads to tiredness, weakness, and aching muscles and joints. Create a good, stable standing posture to give you the starting point for efficient and relaxed movement in all the standing exercises.

How to begin

Stand, with your feet pointing forward about hip-width apart, your hands on your hips and your shoulders as relaxed as possible. Gradually move your body in circles, then forward and backward, and finally to the left and to the right, to find a central, relaxed point.

Here are some simple steps to help you to improve your posture:

1. When walking, make a conscious effort to keep your backbone straight and hold your shoulders back. Pull in your stomach and buttocks and tuck in your chin.

2. When seated, sit up straight, do not cross your legs.

3. If working at a desk choose a seat in which you are comfortable and which is at the correct position for your desk. The seat should be high enough to allow your thighs to rest horizontally on the seat.

4. Wear sensible low-heeled shoes. Keep high ones for the occasional night out. Shoes with low heels put far less strain on your back than stiletto heels.

5. Practice walking around the house with a heavy book balanced on your head, as though you were at a deportment class.

Feet

Focus on your feet. Gently sway your body, backward and forward, from side to side, and round in circles, to distribute your weight more evenly.

Calf muscles

Move your attention to your calf muscles and your shins. Again, shift your weight gently in all directions, noticing how the tension builds and relaxes.

Knees

Concentrate on your kneecaps. Do you feel tension or pressure in these areas? If so, shift your weight gently in all directions until you feel the knees release or unlock.

Thigh muscles

Shift your weight in circles, backward and forward and from side to side, until you feel your thighs relax.

Pelvis and buttocks

This area is the center of your posture. To find a neutral, relaxed position, gently and slowly tip your pelvis forward and backward until you feel the place where there is the least amount of tension.

Stomach wall

Bring your attention to the abdomen. Tighten your stomach muscles as much as possible, then release.

Back

To release tension in your lower back, concentrate on relaxing the area between your buttocks and shoulder blades.

Chest

Take some shallow, then some deep breaths, breathing into your back and the sides of your ribcage. Allow your breath to find a middle depth and breathe in and out five times.

Shoulders

Gently pull your shoulders backward and upward as tightly as you are able to without straining.

Arms

Let your arms hang as dead weights and then gently turn them inward and outward.

Neck

To find a tension-free position for the neck, use forward-bending, backward-bending, looking-right, and looking-left movements. You can also tip your head sideways to the left and right.

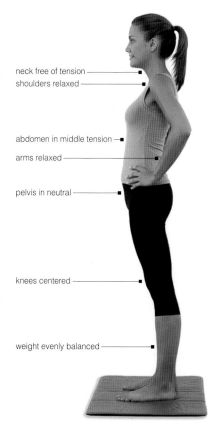

neck free of tension
shoulders relaxed

abdomen in middle tension
arms relaxed

pelvis in neutral

knees centered

weight evenly balanced

Sitting **posture**

This will encourage you to sit in a good relaxed posture. Most people spend a lot of time sitting but tend to slouch rather than sit upright. This exercise helps to retrain the body and you can practice it any time you are sitting down. Occasionally, balance a book on your head (as shown) to check your sitting posture.

1 Sit on the front two-thirds of the chair with your feet placed flat on the floor and hip-width apart. (You can sit with your buttocks against the back of the chair if you are practicing this in your daily life, but moving forward reduces the temptation to lean back.) Drop your shoulders, place your hands on your thighs, and relax your pelvic–floor muscles. Breathe in deeply and widely, projecting your breath into your back and the

sides of your ribcage. Elevate up slightly through your spine to help straighten your posture.

2 Breathe out with control, tightening the muscles of your pelvic floor. Breathe in and release the tension in your pelvic floor, then breathe out, and tighten your pelvic floor again. Breathe in again and release the tension, then breathe out, this time tightening your pelvic–floor muscles to near-capacity tension. Breathe in and then out, then relax. Rest for 30–60 seconds. Repeat three times.

Safety points
- You want your spine to be erect without forcing it.
- Do not hold this position for too long the first few times that you try it. It may take time for you to feel comfortable in a good sitting posture.

You and your **body**

Before you embark on an exercise routine, it is very helpful to have a basic understanding of how your body works, and why it's important to be aware of your current level of fitness before you start. Being muscle-aware will help you to target the areas that you want to firm up.

How your body moves

Your body's framework is the skeleton, made up of more than 200 bones that support your body and allow you to move. Muscles fixed to the ends of bones permit an enormous range of movement. However, joints and muscles that aren't regularly exercised become stiff and immobile, leading to pain and possible injury.

When starting out on your training program, you need to be sure to progress properly:

- Start with the easiest movements and progress gradually to more difficult movements. Don't rush to progress.
- Perform all movements in a slow and controlled manner until coordination, strength, and confidence allow you to make higher-speed movements.

Basic rules when exercising

Whatever your age, before exercising it is important to remember these basic guidelines.

- Exercise at a rate that feels right for you.
- Don't exercise when you feel unwell.
- Always warm up and cool down to prevent injury.
- Don't push yourself too hard—build up gradually.
- Check with your GP if you have any medical condition, especially if you are pregnant.

Body **types**

People generally fall into one of three basic body types—endomorph, mesomorph, or ectomorph—although not everyone fits exactly into one type, and you may combine elements of two. Each body type has its own characteristics and ways of responding to exercise and diet.

Working with your body shape

We all have a unique bone structure and body shape that, frankly, we can't change. Some of us are genetically programed to be very slender (ectomorphs), others are curvaceous with a tendency to gain weight (endomorphs), while others tend to be athletic (mesomorphs). It's important to work out the shape you are before embarking on your fitness routine—if you are a natural endomorph, no amount of exercise or dieting will give you a waiflike, ectomorphic look. Furthermore, women are naturally designed to store fat on the hips and thighs to protect the reproductive organs.

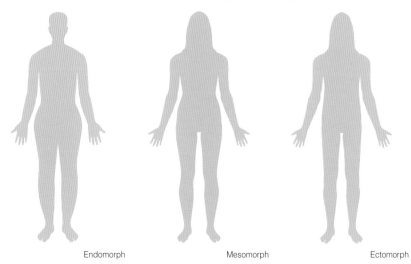

Endomorph   Mesomorph   Ectomorph

Endomorph

If you are an endomorph, your body will tend to be pear-shaped, so that your hips are broader than your shoulders and you have a wide bone structure. You're also more likely to have a curvier body than other types, and may be prone to gaining weight and storing fat. Aerobic exercise can counter this.

Mesomorph

If you are a mesomorph, then you're likely to be of average weight—neither plump nor skinny—and have a shape that falls somewhere between endomorph and ectomorph. Your shoulders may be wider than your hips and you may have a tendency to gain muscle quite easily, but you'll generally have little in the way of body fat. You'll also find it relatively easy to lose weight. A balanced exercise program, which perhaps includes some aerobic activities, is a good option for mesomorphs.

Ectomorph

Typical ectomorphs are thin and have a small frame. Your shoulders and hips will be narrow, you'll have very little body fat, and a narrow chest and stomach. Your legs and arms will also be thin and you will have a narrow face.

Ectomorphs tend to flourish with exercise. However, this body type can be prone to fatigue, and it's important not to attempt too much when you're tired.

Apple and pear

You may have come across the terms "apple" and "pear" to describe body shapes. If you're an apple, then you tend to gain fat in the midsection of the body.

People with pear-shaped bodies tend to store fat below the waistline. Although it's regarded as healthier to be pear-shaped than apple-shaped, the thighs, buttocks, and hips may need extra attention.

Apples and pears

Use the following technique to discover whether you're more of an apple than a pear. You're apple-shaped if the ratio is 0.8 or more for women and 1.0 or more for men. If the ratio is less than 0.8 or 1.0, you have more of a pear shape (endomorph).

1. Place a tape measure directly onto your skin (not over clothes) and measure your waist at the navel and your hips at their widest point.

2. To work out your waist-to-hip ratio, divide the waist measurement by the hip measurement. The result will be your waist-to-hip ratio.

Of course, you may have a neutral body shape that's neither apple- nor pear-shaped. If this sounds like you, then stick to a good exercise routine, eat a healthy, balanced diet, and enjoy your choice of training.

Other fitness **options**

If you want to get fit, then you'll have to include some activity that raises your heartbeat for at least 15 minutes at a time. There are two main types of exercise that will help you achieve fitness: aerobic exercise and toning or strengthening work. Both are important, and there are plenty of options.

Aerobic exercises

These exercises help to burn fat and involve any form of activity that makes you feel a little out of breath. They include cycling, jogging, skipping, power–walking, running, and swimming.

Toning or strengthening exercises

These exercises, like the ones in this book, build up specific muscle groups and, in doing so, increase the rate at which the calories you take in are used up.

Cycling

The idea of squeezing into a pair of Lycra shorts and hitting the roads on your bike may not fill you with an adrenalin rush, but when you consider its health benefits, it is well worth a second thought.

Cycling is an ideal exercise for toning up muscles, getting out in the fresh air,

and just popping out to the shops. If you're new to cycling, it's important to begin slowly and not overdo it, even if you consider yourself to have a good fitness level. Each sport requires a different set of skills and the use of a specific range of

muscles, so being fit in one sport doesn't necessarily mean you'll slip with ease into another. The bike you use should be comfortable, in safe working order, and the right size for your height.

Water aerobics

This is based on normal aerobic exercises like running, jogging, and walking, but the exercises are performed in water, generally at a local swimming pool. It is a perfect form of all-round exercise and the idea is to work the muscles against the resistance of the water.

Swimming

Swimming is one of the least stressful forms of exercise, so it's an ideal choice to complement your exercise program. Plus, you don't need to invest in expensive equipment to begin doing it.

Swimming helps stretch the hamstrings and hips, too, and the action of moving your legs in the water can improve flexibility in your ankles. Aim to swim for up to 30 minutes per session; you can spend more time in the water as fitness levels increase.

Some people love swimming but for those of us who aren't natural swimmers, plowing along at the same pace can become monotonous. Thankfully, there are ways of alleviating the boredom. To provide variety, try alternating between different strokes—one lap of front crawl followed by a lap of backstroke and then butterfly. Or try speeding up your pace for one lap, then slowing down for the next.

Powerwalking

How about taking up powerwalking? Not a gentle saunter around the park but a brisk walk, head and shoulders back, arms swinging, stomach held in, and taking long, determined strides. Not only will it encourage better posture, but powerwalking is also ideal for toning up the thighs, arms, and legs. The more intense you make it, the more calories you will burn up. And when you are powering along, make sure that you take in deep breaths of fresh air.

A healthy **diet**

"You are what you eat" is one of those irritating platitudes that happens to be true. Stuff yourself with junk food or drink too much alcohol and you will feel tired, bloated, and sluggish. Eat a well-balanced diet and you will feel much more alert and full of increased vitality and vigor.

Following the rules

Remember, it doesn't matter how much exercise you do, it can never fully compensate for poor eating habits. The only way to get fit and eliminate surplus fat is to:

- Change your eating habits.
- Increase your level of exercise.

By sticking to these two basic rules, you will be well on your way to achieving that perfect shape.

Nourishing the body

Changing eating habits does not mean that you have to follow a diet and count all your calories. What it does mean is that you should eat healthy, nourishing food containing a balance of essential nutrients, which in turn are derived from the following:

Carbohydrates: These provide energy for the body and come in two basic forms.

Simple carbohydrates basically comprise sugar and very little else. Complex carbohydrates include starchy foods, such as bread, potatoes, cereal, pasta, and rice.

Fats: The number one enemy in terms of a lean body but essential for helping to insulate and protect the organs and nerves. Fats are found in varying quantities in foods such as butter, cheese, lard, snacks, and fatty meat. The basic principle of a healthy diet is to reduce the amount of fat you eat. It doesn't mean cutting fat out totally, but rather choosing those foods sensibly.

Proteins: The body breaks down the protein from food into its component parts, called "amino acids," which it then uses to build and repair tissue and muscle. Protein is found in products such as meat, poultry, fish, dairy foods, eggs, beans, lentils, and nuts.

Minerals: These are vital to the human body as they help to form bones, strengthen teeth, maintain a healthy immune system, and support the vitamins in their work. Calcium, for instance, is important for helping to build strong bones and teeth.

Vitamins: These substances are vital for good health and the maintenance of various bodily functions. A well-balanced diet containing plenty of fresh foods should be rich in vitamins.

Lowfat food

There are several ways to help cut back the fat content of your food:

- Use lowfat or skim milk.
- Whenever possible, steam, broil, or bake food, instead of frying it.
- Use lowfat yogurt instead of cream, ice cream, or other dairy products.
- Eat cottage cheese instead of fullfat cheese.
- Add more fish and poultry to your diet.
- Always trim any visible fat off meat.
- Simmer ingredients in vegetable stock, instead of braising them in lard or butter.

What to eat

The healthiest diet is one that is high in fruit, vegetables, grains, and pulses and low in animal and dairy products.

- Complex carbohydrates should form half your daily diet.
- Eat at least five portions of fruit and vegetables a day.
- Eat oily fish at least once a week.
- Limit your consumption of red meat and cheeses.
- Eat plenty of fiber-rich foods.
- Reduce your salt intake—use in cooking only.
- Limit your sugar intake—try not to use too much in tea and coffee.
- Eat fresh foods whenever possible and cut back on processed foods.

Chest and back

In this section you will find basic standing and sitting exercises to improve the muscles in the chest and back. Some are traditional exercises or established moves from exercise systems, such as yoga and Pilates, and focus on toning and strengthening exercises for the upper body.

Introduction

To keep the chest and back healthy and enable your body to perform a full range of movements, three things are necessary: mobility of the spine, supple muscles, and strength. All these can be achieved by doing moderate exercise regularly and correctly and by following the general advice in this book.

The benefits

Doing specific back exercises will help you to ensure that you are working all the important muscle groups. Regular movement helps to maintain the elasticity of the muscles and it builds their power. It also serves to keep the joints mobile. Movement encourages good circulation of blood and other fluids around the body. This helps to keep the joints lubricated and allows muscles and joints to take in nutrients and to expel waste products.

Improving your upper body

Achieving a supertoned body requires a combination of two forms of exercise: the first is toning, as described in this book, and the other is aerobic. The aerobic form of activity will help to burn off any excess body fat as well as improve your cardiovascular health.

About your upper body muscles

A key to maintaining stability in the upper body is correct use of the deepest abdominal

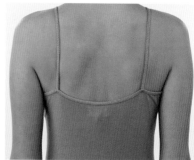

muscle—the transversus abdominis. This muscle is just below your navel and runs in a band from one side of the abdomen to the other. When you contract this muscle, it takes the pressure off the spine.

The abdominal muscles work with the muscles of the back to support and stabilize the spine. Also important are the hip flexors (psoas), which run from the upper part of the thigh bone to the lumbar vertebrae, and the hamstrings.

The back muscles

The muscles of the back are arranged in several layers. The superficial muscles are mainly broad sheets of muscles that connect the vertebrae to the shoulder blades and joints. The middle layer consists of strap-shaped muscles that run over the lower ribs, chest, and lower back. The deepest muscles run from one vertebra to another, helping to keep them in position.

Middle and lower back

The latissimus dorsi is the largest muscle in the upper body and covers the middle and lower back.

Chest muscles

The pectoralis major is a large, fan-shaped muscle, which has several attachments. One portion fastens to the middle and inner parts of your collarbone, working with the

front of your shoulder to move your arms in front, above, and rotate them inward. The other part attaches to your breastbone and ribs—this muscle is activated by moving your arms only in a downward or forward movement of both arms.

What you'll need

For this section you'll need a chair, a non-slip mat, and a towel. Don't forget to warm up and cool down!

Warming-up **exercises**

It is always essential to warm up before undertaking any form of exercise. Choose a couple of the exercises shown over the next few pages and spend a little time warming up. You should allow around ten minutes for this, and alternate them so you don't get bored.

Rolling down

This will mobilize the spine and will benefit the spine, shoulders, and upper body.

1 Stand upright with your spine in neutral. Place your feet hip-width apart, keep your knees soft, and let your arms hang loosely by your sides.

2 Gently nod your chin toward your chest, then roll forward, keeping the ribcage soft and rolling toward the hips. Sense each vertebra rolling, one at a time.

3 Only roll down to your point of comfort—do not try to go too far too soon, or you will strain yourself. At the bottom of the move, inhale, feeling the air inflate your spine and keeping the pelvic-floor muscles and abdominals engaged.

4 Roll back up, nice and gently. As you finish the roll, exhale and release the shoulder blades. At first, do the roll five times, increasing to a maximum of ten.

1

2

C-curve warm-up

This exercise will help to mobilize the spine and strengthen the central and back muscles.

1 Sit on the floor, with your knees bent, your weight evenly distributed.

2 Place your hands lightly behind your knees, but do not pull on your hands as you carry out the move.

3 Exhale, and rock backward off the pelvis toward the floor.

1

2

4 Pause, inhale, and return to the upright starting position. Keep the abdominals scooped and hollowed throughout the whole move for support. Only go as far as you can each time without lifting your feet off the floor. Repeat the movement five times, increasing to a maximum of ten.

Pivot

This mobilizes the whole body and promotes coordination.

1 Stand upright with your spine in neutral. Place your feet wider than hip-width apart, keep your knees soft, and let your arms hang loosely by your sides. Inhale.

2 Exhale, and twist your body to one side. Let your arms swing loosely, moving with you. Your legs will also twist with the movement.

3 Inhale, and slowly twist back to the center; exhale, and twist to the other side; and then inhale, and twist back to the center.

4 Each time you twist, raise your arms higher, until they reach over your head, then work them back down to your sides, in a continuous, flowing movement. Take three twists in each direction to get to the top of the movement, and three more twists in each direction to get back down.

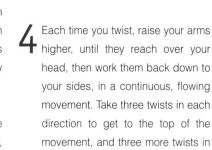

Back twists

Gentle back twists from a standing position are easy to control; it is hard to push yourself too far. They give the spine a satisfying stretch, rotating the vertebrae and working the muscles of the back.

1 Stand tall, with your feet hip-width apart. Put your hands on your hips.

2 Slowly turn to the right as far as you comfortably can. Start the turn from the hips, lifting the spine upward as you turn. Keep the neck and head in line with the spine—don't try to turn the head further, since this will put pressure on the neck. Hold the twist for a few moments, breathing normally.

3 Slowly turn back to the center. Then repeat on the other side.

WATCH POINT
Try to coordinate your breathing with the movement. Take a deep breath in before you turn, then twist as you breathe out. Return to the center on an out-breath, too. This helps you to control the movement.

2

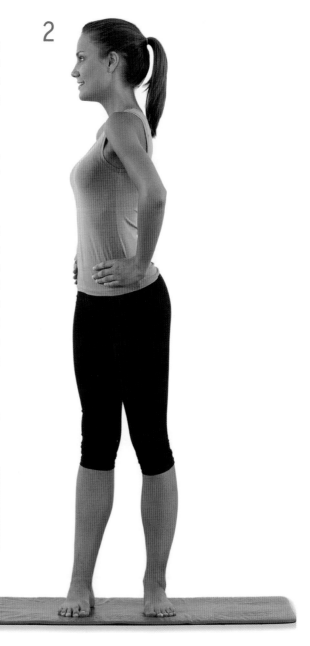

Introductory **exercises**

These first-stage exercises are aimed at beginners, so you should find them relatively easy to start with, allowing you to become more involved as you progress. If you find any of the exercises a bit too difficult, simply replace them with something else of the same level.

Easy plank (tension hold)

Holding your body in a three-quarter plank shape strengthens the deep transverse muscles that cross the stomach area. Keeping your knees on the floor makes this exercise much easier than the traditional plank, which you can progress to during the advanced exercises.

1 Adopt a traditional press-up position but keep your knees on the floor and your feet in the air.

2 Keep your shoulder blades drawn into your back and make sure you don't dip in the middle or raise your buttocks in the air. Hold this position for a count of ten, breathing regularly throughout.

1

C-curve

This is a progression of the warm-up exercise. This time, position your hands lightly on the sides of your knees. Try to unroll further each time you practice the movement, but only go as far as you can comfortably.

1 Sit on the floor, with your weight evenly distributed and your spine in neutral. Relax your shoulders, with the shoulder blades melting down your back.

1

2 Inhale, and with the points of your toes gently touching the floor, slowly roll backward off the pelvis. Rock slightly back and forth.

3 Balancing on your toes, exhale as you roll back to the start position.

MODIFICATION
Relax your feet and lift your toes, resting only your heels on the floor (this will take the tension out of your hip flexors).

2

Standing wall press-up

This exercise is a fantastic way to build upper body strength as well as tone through the back of your upper arm muscles and into your chest.

1 Stand at arm's length away from a wall, with your feet shoulder-width apart. Place your hands against the wall, with your arms stretched out in front of you and your fingers pointing to the ceiling.

2 Keeping your back straight and your head looking straight in front of you, slowly bend your arms at the elbows.

3 Aim to lower yourself a little way toward the wall and then push back to your start position.

WATCH POINT
If you want to increase the level of difficulty, try moving your legs further back. Also, keeping your abdominal muscles pulled in will help tone your stomach muscles.

Bust lift

This exercise targets the chest muscle, which is responsible for supporting the bust. If this muscle is not exercised it will become less supportive, which means the bust begins to droop. This is a great way of toning and giving yourself a bust lift.

1 Stand upright with good posture, knees slightly bent, feet hip-width apart, and stomach pulled in.

2 Extend your arms out in front of you at chest height, bend the elbows, and join the hands by the palms facing into each other.

3 Stay in this position, press into your palms, and, holding this squeeze, slowly lift your palms a little bit higher. Hold for a second while still applying the squeeze, then slowly lower to the start position; release the squeeze for a second, then reapply and lift.

Bell pull

This exercise works on toning your arms through your biceps and triceps as well as toning your chest muscle. This is great for women, as it helps lift and tone the bust as well as giving the arms a fabulous workout.

1 Stand with good posture, knees slightly bent, and your feet hip-width apart.

2 Lift your arms to shoulder height and then bend at the elbows, so that your arms form an L-shape. Press your arms together and keep elbows at shoulder height.

3 Take a deep breath in and then, as you breathe out, gently lift your arms a little bit higher, hold for a second, then lower slowly again.

WATCH POINT
To get your abdominal muscles working, make sure you keep your stomach pulled in tight to your spine. Also, be sure not to arch your back.

Criss-cross arms

This simple exercise tones your triceps, biceps, and chest muscles.

1 Sit with good posture, arms extended out in front of you, palms facing each other.

2 Cross your right arm over the left, turning your palms down along the way. Pause, then return to the start position.

3 Do all your repetitions on one arm and repeat on the other arm.

> **WATCH POINT**
> *Focus on keeping your abdominal muscles pulled in throughout. To make this more of a challenge, try using weights.*

Advanced **exercises**

Now that you've worked through the introductory exercises and are feeling fitter and more confident, you can progress to this second series of exercises. As before, if you find any particular exercises difficult, simply replace them with something else from this level.

Plank

This doesn't sound or look too taxing but, if you do it right, you'll find that it's a very intense exercise, and highly effective at toning the abdominal muscles.

1 Lie on your front, resting your forehead on the backs of your hands.

2 Keeping your elbows bent, slide your hands across the floor, rotating from the shoulders, until you find your perfect "press-up" position either side of your chest.

3 Curl your toes underneath you and push up off the floor with your hands. Keep your elbows soft to stop them locking, and keep your neck and head relaxed and in line with your spine.

4 Hold the pose for ten seconds, then gently lower yourself back down to the floor again. Remember to breathe during the exercise.

Super chest toner

This is a great exercise to work deep into the chest muscles, which can help to support and lift the bust muscle, as well as increase your range of flexibility through your shoulders.

1 Lie on the mat, face up, with your knees bent and feet firmly on the floor.

2 Using a weight in each hand, bend your arms out to the side so that they rest on the floor, elbows in line with your shoulders and bent, to form an L-shape.

3 Slowly lift your arms off the floor while maintaining the bend and aim to bring both arms to meet directly in line with your face. Hold for a couple of seconds, then slowly lower back to the floor, and repeat.

> **WATCH POINT**
> *By keeping your navel pulled down to your spine, you will protect your back throughout this workout. Doing this will also tone your abdominal muscles.*

Front-lying chest lift

The front-lying chest lift is usually used as part of a yoga pose. It's great for stretching out all the muscles across the chest, including the "pecs."

1 Lie face down on the floor with your palms on the floor either side of your chest and your legs stretched out behind you.

2 Keeping your hips and thighs on the floor, push up with your hands and arms so that your chest is off the floor. Don't come up too far—aim to lift your chest just a short distance off the floor.

3 Hold the pose for ten seconds, then release and return to the starting position.

> **WATCH POINT**
> *Some of you may find it hard to arch the back as you lift yourself up into the pose—it depends how flexible you already are. If you can't lift your chest far off the floor, don't abandon this stretch—it will get easier over time.*

2

Dumb-bell row

Doing this exercise is like starting a lawnmower. It targets the muscles in the middle of the back, such as the trapezius. So if you practice this religiously, it will make wearing backless dresses all the more appealing.

1 Rest your right knee and your right hand on the seat of a chair.

2 Holding a dumbbell or tin of soup in your left hand, pull it back toward your hip.

3 Extend your left arm diagonally out in front of you, so that it travels toward the ground.

4 Bring the dumbbell back to your hip and repeat the movement.

2

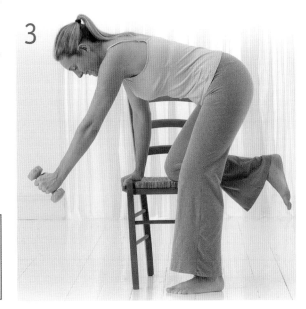

3

WATCH POINT
You should do this exercise on one side at a time if you have a bad back. If you want to work both sides at once, take away the chair and stand in a squat position while doing the exercise.

Cooling-down **exercises**

Just as you need to warm up the body for exercising, you also need to cool it down after you have finished. Try the two exercises shown on this spread, and take the time to cool down properly. Ideally, you should look to spend around ten minutes doing this.

Post-exercise chest stretch

This stretch will help encourage deep breathing, which will enable you to feel a whole lot perkier and more refreshed in the morning.

1 Sit comfortably on the mat, cross-legged, and with good posture. Lift your arms out to the sides and place them behind you.

2 Keep the shoulders down as you clasp your hands together.

3 Hold this stretch for 20 seconds.

2

Post-exercise upper back stretch

You will feel this stretch across your shoulders and the deep muscles of the back. Do not overstretch, as this should be a gentle movement.

1 Sit comfortably on the mat, cross-legged, and with good posture. Lift up your arms in front of you.

2 Clasp your hands in front of you and imagine you are hugging a large ball. Feel the stretch in your back.

3 Hold this stretch for 20 seconds.

2

Train your brain

Use your mind to help you get the most from your workout. Focus on what you are doing correctly. As you are exercising, tell yourself how well you are doing. Think of each muscle contracting and stretching as you do your routine. This can make you do even better, whereas concentrating on what you are doing wrong sets you up to fail. You can even use visualizations to convince yourself that your body is becoming fitter and more toned!

Arms and shoulders

This chapter targets the key areas of your upper body. It will banish any wobble from your arms, tone your shoulders, and define and strengthen your back. Don't worry—these exercises won't bulk out your muscles, but will lengthen and define them, improve your posture, naturally lift your bust, and boost your confidence, too!

Introduction

The arms and upper body comprise an area that is often overlooked when undertaking exercise routines. This can result in the muscles becoming weak and saggy, which may lead to poor posture and even health problems. Follow these exercises to improve strength and tone and see the difference in no time.

The benefits

By exercising your arms and upper body you can achieve an incredibly toned and svelte shape. Working on your upper body also helps to realign your muscles, which will improve your strength, enhance your posture, and immediately make you look slimmer and more confident.

Your arms and upper body contain some major muscle groups, so working on this area will naturally raise your metabolic rate. As well as toning and increasing your strength, you will also be "melting away" any excess calories by working harder.

The muscles of the arms and shoulders

It helps to have a basic understanding of the muscles you need to work on to exercise the arms and shoulders.

Upper arms: The biceps is the muscle that runs down the front of your upper

arm. It allows you to flex your elbow and rotate your forearm so that your palms can face down. This muscle is attached to the shoulder joint and your elbow joint.

The muscle at the back of the upper arm is called the triceps. It is attached to the shoulder and the elbow and it is activated by straightening through the arm. This muscle can easily lose its tone and is often referred to as "flabby arms" or "bat wing arms."

Shoulders: The muscles that form your shoulders are known as the deltoids and consist of three sections, or heads. Each of these sections has different actions:

- The anterior (front) originates at the collarbone and moves your arms up and forward, as well as rotating inward.

- The lateral (side) head works primarily to lift your arms to the side and assist the anterior and posterior heads in their movements.

- The posterior (back) head attaches to your shoulder blade and moves your arms to the rear as well as rotating them.

What you need

Some of the exercises require hand weights. These come in different sizes so you can lift slightly heavier ones as you increase your upper body fitness. If you don't have any weights, a can of soup makes a good dumbbell because it's easy to hold. It is a good idea to perform your exercises in front of a mirror so that you can assess your technique.

Controlling your movements

Make sure that all exercises are performed slowly, carefully, and with your full attention. You really do need to concentrate on what you're doing and think about how your body is responding to any exercise.

Warming-up **exercises**

It is always essential to warm up before undertaking any form of exercise. Choose a couple of the exercises shown over the next few pages and spend a little time warming up. You should allow around ten minutes for this, and alternate them so you don't get bored.

Shoulder rolls

This will ensure that you have fully warmed through the shoulders and chest and mobilized into the shoulder joint.

1 Stand with good posture and check that your feet are slightly wider than hip-width apart.

2 Make sure that your knees are slightly bent and that your abdominal muscles are pulled in tight toward your spine.

3 Very slowly and gently, start to rotate through your shoulders by lifting your shoulders up, then behind. Each time, increase this movement and aim to make the circles bigger.

4 Repeat the exercise ten times.

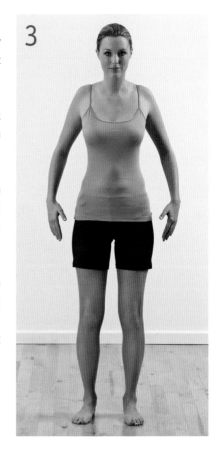

3

Deltoid stretch

You may find this stretch a little difficult to do at first, but just stretch as far as you find comfortable to start with.

1 Stand with good posture, extend one arm out in front of you, and cross it in front of the mid-line of your body.

2 Keep both your shoulders facing forward. Support the stretching arm on the fleshy part of the forearm.

3 Hold this stretch on each arm for ten seconds.

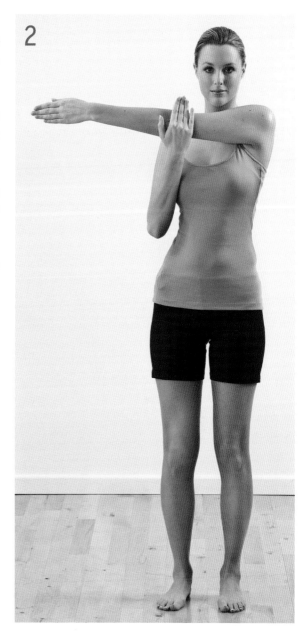

2

Shrugs

This will help to release tension from the neck and shoulders.

1 Stand upright with your shoulder girdle and spine in neutral. Place your feet hip-width apart, keep your knees soft, and let your arms hang loosely by your sides. Focus on your breathing, with eyes closed if you wish.

2 Inhale, and lift your shoulders up toward your ears.

3 Exhale, and draw the shoulder blades into neutral. At first, do the shrugs five times, increasing to a maximum of ten.

1

2

3

Arm swing

This will increase the flexibility of your chest muscles and help to loosen your upper back.

1 Stand with good posture, knees bent, and stomach pulled in.

2 Lift both arms out to either side of your body.

3 In a slow and controlled manner, bring both arms in front so they cross over, then back out to either side.

4 Be sure to keep your abdominal muscles pulled in to maintain good posture throughout.

5 Repeat the exercise ten times.

Mind over matter

Get the most from your workout by focusing on what you are doing as you are exercising, and tell yourself how well you are doing. You can even use visualizations as you exercise to convince yourself that your body is becoming fitter and more toned!

3

Introductory **exercises**

These first-stage exercises are aimed at beginners, so you should find them relatively easy to start with, allowing you to become more involved as you progress. If you find any of the exercises a bit too difficult, simply replace them with something else of the same level.

3

2

Biceps curl

The biceps are the muscles at the front of the upper arms. They are relatively easy to tone, so practicing this exercise will help to give you shapely arms that you'll want to show off.

1 Stand up tall, with feet hip-width apart, and knees soft.

2 Extend your arms out in front of you with palms facing upward, holding a can of soup or a dumbbell in each hand.

3 Bend your elbows and bring both your hands in toward your shoulders so that your arms form right angles. Reverse the movement so that your elbows are fully extended in front of you again. Keep your elbows soft at all times.

Triceps squeeze back

This is an easy-to-perform standing exercise that will tone through the back of your upper arms, creating a long, toned triceps muscle and banishing any wobbly arms. The other great thing with this exercise is that it also stretches your chest muscles, which helps promote good posture.

1 Stand with good posture and your knees slightly bent. Hold the weights, keeping your arms by your side, with your palms facing away from you backward.

2 Lift your chest up and pull your shoulders back.

3 Lift both arms directly behind you, and feel this working through your triceps. Hold your arms at the highest point, then slowly lower back to the start position.

WATCH POINT
This is a small lift, so don't expect to raise your arms too high. Keep your knees slightly bent and your abdominal muscles pulled in tight.

4

Front raises

This exercise will sculpt your shoulders and create tone and definition through the front of your arms.

1 Stand with good posture, your feet hip-width apart, and knees soft.

2 Keep your abdominal muscles tight and chest relaxed.

3 Hold a weight in each hand with palms facing in, weights by your thighs.

4 In a slow and controlled smooth move, lift both arms up forward and straight to shoulder height, then slowly lower both arms back to the start position.

Lifting weights

When lifting weights, always keep the movement slow and controlled. This not only works the muscles harder, but it also prevents any injuries occurring.

Front arm toner (hammer curl)

This tones through the front of your upper arms and also works on strengthening your forearm muscles.

1 Stand with your feet shoulder-width apart, knees soft, elbows fixed, and stomach pulled in tight to promote good upper body posture.

2 With a weight in each hand, let both arms hang down long by the side of your body, fully straightened with your palms facing in toward your body.

3 Simultaneously, lift your weights upward, without moving your elbows, hold for a second, then slowly lower back to your start position.

2
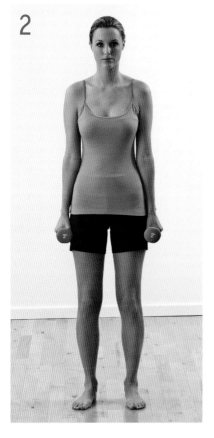

3

Superwoman arms

This will tone through your shoulders and biceps, while working to improve the flexibility of your shoulder joints.

1 Kneel on the mat on all fours, with your wrists directly under your shoulders, and your knees under your hips on the mat. Keep your abdominal muscles contracted.

Holding a small weight, lift up one arm so that it is in line with your shoulder.

2 Now slowly bend the arm back so that your elbow is in line with your shoulder. Hold, then gently release back to a straight arm and repeat. Do all your repetitions on one arm and then repeat on the other arm.

Kneeling boxed press-up

This exercise targets lots of your upper body and arm muscles, so it is great for toning your arms, your bust, and also for building upper body strength. You will notice that the fitter and the more toned your arms become, the stronger you will be, and you should soon be able to perform these with ease.

1 Kneel on the mat with knees directly under your hips. Hands should be slightly wider than shoulder-width apart, with fingers pointing forward.

2 Keep your body weight over your hands, stomach pulled in tight and your back flat. Slowly lower your body so your elbows are at a 90-degree angle.

3 Gently push yourself back up to the start position.

Advanced **exercises**

Now that you've worked through the introductory exercises and are feeling fitter and more confident, you can progress to this second series of exercises. As before, if you find any particular exercises difficult, simply replace them with something else from this level.

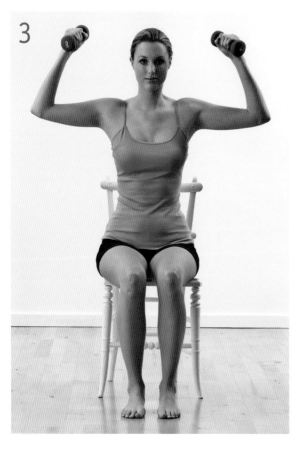

3

Arms out biceps curl

This exercise tones your biceps as well as engaging your triceps, as this muscle has to stabilize the arms in the exercise position.

1 Sit on your chair with good upright body posture, knees bent, and feet firmly on the floor, slightly apart.

2 Using a weight in each hand, lift both arms, fully extended, out to your sides, to shoulder height. Turn your palms so that they face upward.

3 Keeping your stomach muscles pulled in, slowly bend your elbows. Aim for your hands to reach your shoulders, hold, then slowly straighten your arms back out.

> **WATCH POINT**
> *Try to focus on just bending through the elbows and aim to keep the shoulder joint very still.*

Triceps kick-back

This exercise isolates the back of the upper arm, specifically targeting the troublesome area sometimes referred to as "flabby arms" or "bat wing arms."

1 Kneel over a chair, with one arm supporting your body and one knee bent on the chair. Ensure that the elbow of the supporting arm stays soft and that the knee of the leg extended to the floor is also soft.

2 With your weight in one hand, position your upper arm so it is parallel to the floor and bent at the elbow.

3 Slowly extend the arm until it is straight, then slowly return and repeat. Do all your repetitions on one arm and then repeat on the other arm, by turning around and placing your opposite leg on the chair.

> **WATCH POINT**
> *For a greater range of motion, the upper arm can be positioned with the elbow at a slightly higher angle than the shoulder.*

Circles in the air

This exercise is great for general toning of the arms and shoulders. Using weights will also help to develop strength in the arms and have a pumping effect on the muscles, so that you'll look great in short-sleeved tops.

1 Stand with feet hip-width apart, knees slightly bent and arms resting by your sides.

2 With a dumbbell in each hand, cross your arms in front of each other level with your hips.

3 Next, circle them up toward the ceiling so that they cross over in the air above your head. Then bring them back round to the start position.

4 Pause for one second, then repeat the movement in the opposite direction.

Triceps bend

This is a fantastic exercise for creating tone and definition through your back arms, as it isolates the triceps muscle that is found at the back of the upper arms. This muscle is toned by extending your arms straight from a bent position.

1 Lie on your back on the mat with your knees bent. Hold a weight in each hand.

2 Extend the arms straight up over your chest, palms facing in toward each other, ensuring that you have a firm grip of the weights.

3 Slowly bend your elbows and lower your hands down to a few inches above your forehead, to form a 90-degree angle.

4 Squeeze the triceps muscle by slowly straightening your arms, without locking out your joints.

Cooling-down **exercises**

Just as you need to warm up the body for exercising, you also need to cool it down after you have finished. Try the two exercises shown on this spread, and take the time to cool down properly. Ideally, you should look to spend around ten minutes doing this.

Triceps stretch

Your triceps muscles are found at the back of the top of your arms. Giving them a good stretch will boost circulation and help to get rid of any blotchy, pimply skin that may reside there.

1 Stand with good posture, lift one arm above your head and drop the palm of the hand behind the head between the shoulder blades.

2 Lift the other arm and support the stretching arm on the soft, fleshy part of the upper arm or just above the elbow.

3 Hold this stretch for 15 seconds. Repeat on the other arm.

Inner arm stretch

This is an easy stretch to do, and will really get your shoulders loosened up. It's great to do if you've been particularly stressed-out recently, because it will help to get rid of any built-up tension.

1 Stand in an open doorway, with your abs tight and body straight.

2 Hold on to the doorframe with your left hand just below shoulder level, or as high as is comfortable. Take a big step forward so your left arm is extended out behind you. Keeping your hips facing forward and your head and neck in line with your spine, rotate your upper body to the right until you feel the stretch in your left arm. Lean forward to feel a greater stretch.

3 Hold for two sets of ten seconds, then turn around, step forward, and repeat the stretch with your right arm.

> **WATCH POINT**
> *Don't worry if you find it difficult to get your arm up to shoulder height, because you can still achieve a good stretch by having it slightly lower.*

2

Stomach

Most of us would love to have a flatter stomach but just can't face the thought of hours and hours of strenuous sit-ups. Well, the good news is you don't have to do this—the key to a fit and toned stomach is to exercise little and often. Just follow the routines in this section and you'll have a flatter stomach within weeks.

Introduction

As well as looking fantastic, a flat stomach increases your flexibility, improves posture, and helps keep the body in good working order. Strengthening the stomach muscles can even help lower the risk of heart disease, high blood pressure, and diabetes. A flat stomach is basically an all-round winner!

The benefits

Apart from the obvious benefit of improving your appearance, firming and toning up your stomach muscles will improve your posture and balance, and increase your flexibility. Building muscle tone doesn't happen overnight, but the varied range of exercises in this section means that you won't become bored or burned out.

Stomach muscles explained

It helps to have a basic understanding of which muscles you need to work on, to make your stomach become more toned and appear flatter.

There are four abdominal muscle groups, which form a natural corset around the middle. They support your lower back, protect internal organs and enable you to bend, twist, and sit up. The deepest of the abdominal muscles is the transversus abdominis, which wraps horizontally around your waist and keeps your lower back stable. The rectus abdominis runs from the pubic bone to the bottom of the ribcage. This muscle enables your trunk to bend and is important for maintaining your posture.

The external and internal obliques run up the sides of your body and enable you to bend to the side and twist your spine. The exercises in this section will work to strengthen all these muscles for a firmer, flatter, fabulously toned stomach.

Effective exercising

When you start out, make sure you don't overdo it—just do as many reps as you can comfortably achieve. To make it effective, it's important that you don't stop for more than a minute between exercises.

Handy hints for a flabby stomach

Learning how to pull your abdominal muscles in can help strengthen them.
- With the stomach muscles relaxed, measure and cut a length of ribbon or string to fit the waist and tie it around.
- As you breathe out, pull the navel in. The objective is to keep any tension off the string by maintaining this hold. Take five breaths, then exhale. Repeat eight times.

Practice makes perfect and this isn't easy, but when you have achieved holding your stomach in flat, without relying on the string, it will come as second nature, even when exercising. Ultimately, this will ensure that you get the best from every workout.

Eating for a flat stomach

Adopting a few healthy eating tips can help beat bloating and boost the effects of exercise.

Don't ever skimp on liquids if you think it could ward off bloating, because drinking lots of water actually promotes a flat stomach by flushing toxins from your system and curbing your appetite. If your body feels starved of water then it will hold on to what there is, which can lead to water retention and the appearance of bloating.

Drink at least eight glasses a day, but don't drink a lot before exercise because it will put pressure on your bladder. You'll know you're well hydrated by checking the color of your urine—the paler it is, the better.

If your stomach has a noticeable wobble, you will have to do some regular cardiovascular exercise to promote fat loss and these healthy eating tips will also help:
- Eat little and often and make sure you have a varied diet. Keep wheat products to a minimum because they can cause bloating and wind.
- Say goodbye to sodas—even if they're "diet" or caffeine-free, they can still cause bloating because they are loaded with gassy bubbles.
- Avoid processed food and ready meals. They are usually laden with salt, sugar, and chemicals, and can upset your stomach's bacterial balance and cause bloating.
- Cut down on salt—it can encourage fluid retention.

What you'll need

You'll need a sturdy chair, a nonslip mat, a cushion, and a pillow or towel to support your head and neck.

Warming-up **exercises**

It is always essential to warm up before undertaking any form of exercise. Choose a couple of the exercises shown over the next few pages and spend a little time warming up. You should allow around ten minutes for this, and alternate them so you don't get bored.

1

Waist twist

It's important not to move your hips and knees during this exercise.

1 Stand up straight with your spine in neutral, and your knees slightly bent (soft, rather than "locked"). Keep your feet hip-width apart and your hands resting on your hips. Make sure your spine is in the neutral position.

2 Tighten your abdominal muscles by pulling your navel back toward your spine.

3 Keeping your hips and knees still, rotate your shoulders and head to the right, then return to the center.

4 Now twist to the left, rotating your head and shoulders, and keeping your hips and knees still. Repeat this exercise five times more on each side.

Hip circles

This exercise will mobilize your lower abdominal muscles. Try to make sure that only your pelvis is rocking, rather than moving your torso.

1 Stand up straight with your knees slightly bent, feet hip-width apart, hands resting on your hips.

2 Tighten your abdominal muscles by gently pulling your navel toward your spine. This movement should feel light and subtle—do not suck in your waist or hold your breath.

3 Gently rotate your pelvis to the right so that you are rotating in a full circle.

4 Repeat nine times to the right, then circle ten times to the left.

3

3

Forward bend

With this exercise, bend only as far as is comfortable—you don't have to touch your toes. Remember, you'll be able to stretch further as time goes by and you become more supple with exercise.

1 Stand up straight with your feet hip-width apart and your knees slightly bent, rather than locked. Place your hands palms downward on the front of your thighs.

2 Tighten your abdominal muscles by gently pulling in your navel toward your backbone.

3 Slowly slide your hands down your legs toward your toes. Try not to overarch your back.

4 Position yourself so you feel a stretch in the hamstrings at the back of your legs, but don't stretch so far that it hurts.

5 Hold for a count of three, then return to the center.

6 Repeat five more times. Keep your breathing steady throughout.

Side bends

Do not do this exercise quickly with your arms above your head, because this will make it hard to control the movement.

1 Stand up straight with your feet hip-width apart and your knees slightly bent, your arms by your sides.

2 Tighten your abdominal muscles by gently pulling your navel toward your spine.

3 Keeping your back straight and without leaning forward, slowly bend to one side from the waist so that your hand slides down the side of your leg. Straighten up again.

4 Repeat on the other side. Repeat five more times on both sides.

WATCH POINT
Never stretch to the point of pain.

3

Introductory **exercises**

These first-stage exercises are aimed at beginners so you should find them relatively easy to start with, allowing you to become more involved as you progress. If you find any of the exercises a bit too difficult, simply replace them with something else of the same level.

Belly tightener

This is also known as "abdominal hollowing" and helps to shorten the abdominal muscles, which is good for your posture and creates the appearance of a flatter stomach.

1 Kneel down on all fours (the "box" position) with your hands shoulder-width apart, your elbows slightly bent and your knees under your hips. Keep your head in line with the rest of your body and look down at the floor, making sure that your chin isn't tucked into your chest.

2 Relax your abdominal muscles, then slowly draw in your navel toward your spine.

3 Hold the muscles in for a count of ten, then slowly relax. Remember to breathe slowly and steadily throughout this exercise.

WATCH POINT
Pull up the abdomen by using your deep abdominal muscles, not by arching your spine.

2

Side reach

The small, controlled movements in this exercise work your stomach muscles even harder.

1 Lie on your back with your spine in neutral, your knees bent, feet flat on the floor, hip-width apart, and palms down, and by your sides. Tighten your abdominal muscles.

2 Lift your head and shoulders off the floor to an angle of 30 degrees. Hold this position and reach out with your right hand toward your right calf.

3 Gently move back and forth ten times, then curl back down again. Remember to breathe regularly throughout.

4 Now repeat this exercise, reaching out with the left hand toward the left calf. Gradually, build up the number of reaches you can do.

Spine rotation

This exercise gently mobilizes your spine, preparing it for harder exercises to come.

1 Sit forward on a chair with your back straight and your hands resting on your thighs. Your knees should be over your ankles.

2 Tighten your abdominal muscles. Keeping your hips and knees forward, slowly rotate your upper body to the left until you can put both hands on the back of the chair. Hold for a count of ten, then return to the center. Repeat the exercise, twisting to the right.

Don't exercise if...

- you are feeling unwell—your body will need all its strength to fight off any infection.
- you have an injury—you might make things worse.
- you have an ongoing medical condition or are on medication—consult your doctor first.
- you've just had a big meal.
- you've been drinking alcohol.

Reverse curl

Reverse curls give a good workout to the transversus abdominis, the deepest abdominal muscle that wraps around your waist like a corset, and the rectus abdominis, the stomach muscle that's responsible for the six-pack look.

1 Lie on your back with your spine in neutral, your arms by your sides, palms facing downward. Tuck your knees in toward your stomach and cross your ankles.

2 Tighten your abdominal muscles by gently pulling your navel in toward your spine.

3 Roll your knees toward your chest and then lower them.

Leg slide

Another easy exercise for tightening your stomach muscles.

1 Lie on your back with your knees bent, your feet flat on the floor, and your arms by your sides, palms facing the floor. You can put a flat pillow or towel under your neck for support if you like.

2 Tighten your abdominal muscles by gently pulling in your navel toward your backbone.

3 Gently tilt your pelvis so that the pelvic bone rises.

4 Raising the toes of one foot, breathe out while sliding your leg forward as far as it will go, with your heel on the floor.

5 Hold for a count of three, then return to the start position, and repeat using the other leg.

How muscles work

Here's the science: muscles are made up of millions of tiny protein filaments that relax and contract to produce movement. Most muscles are attached to bones by tendons and are consciously controlled by your brain. Electrical signals from the brain travel via nerves to the muscles, causing the cells within the muscle to contract. Movement happens when muscles pull on tendons, which move the bones at the joints. Muscles work in pairs, enabling bones to move in two directions. Most movements require the use of several muscle groups.

Abdominal curl

These exercises will tone the rectus abdominis muscle, which runs down the front of your stomach. As you lift your head and shoulders this muscle contracts at both ends. Avoid these exercises if you have neck problems.

1 Lie on your back with a firm, flat pillow or a small towel underneath your head. Keep your feet hip-width apart, parallel and firmly on the floor, and your knees bent. Rest your hands on your thighs.

2 Set your spine to the neutral position and tighten your abdominal muscles. Flex your spine to lift your head and shoulders gently, about 30 degrees off the floor. Your hands will slide up toward your knees as you curl. Keep your lower back in contact with the floor at all times. Slowly curl back down in a continuous movement.

3 To make this harder, put your hands across your chest as you curl. When this becomes easy, you can place your hands at the sides of your head to increase the resistance against which you are working.

> **WATCH POINT**
> *Never put your hands behind your neck when performing curls as you may tug on your neck muscles and strain your neck vertebrae.*

Advanced **exercises**

Now that you've worked through the introductory exercises and are feeling fitter and more confident, you can progress to this second series of exercises. As before, if you find any particular exercises difficult, simply replace them with something else from this level.

Crunches

This is an intense workout for your stomach muscles and a great way of getting washboard-flat abs.

1 Lie on the floor, knees bent, and feet apart, flat on the floor in line with your hips. Make sure that your lower back is pressed into the floor. Put your hands behind your head to support your neck.

2 Engage your stomach muscles, by pulling your abdominals toward your spine, and lift your upper body off the floor as far as you can without arching your lower back. You may find that you can't get up very high, but it's the effort of moving that counts, so make sure that you're pushing yourself as hard as you comfortably can. With practice, you may be able to sit up completely.

3 When you can't go any further, pause for one second. Then gently lower yourself back down into the start position.

WATCH POINT
Make sure you don't use your neck to pull yourself up.

WATCH POINT
Don't use your hands to lift your head off the floor—let your stomach muscles do all the work.

3

Side lift

This exercise works the obliques and reinforces your body's natural alignment. Make sure you don't use the supporting arm to push yourself up—the movement is controlled by the stomach muscles.

1 Lie on your side in a straight line. Extend your lower arm above your head in line with your body. Bend your top arm in front to support you—your hand should be in line with your chest.

2 Tighten your abdominal muscles, then lift both legs together off the floor.

3 Now raise your upper leg higher, keeping it aligned with the bottom leg.

4 Hold for a count of two, then lower the top leg to the bottom leg.

5 Lower both legs slowly to the floor. Repeat on the other side of your body.

WATCH POINT
Both these exercises are great waist-whittlers but you may find them too hard if you're a beginner—you should be able to do these after a few weeks of stomach-toning exercise.

Lower abdominal raise

This is a harder exercise that will really work your abdominal muscles. If it seems easy, then you're not doing it properly!

1 Lie on your back with your knees bent, feet flat on the floor, and hip-width apart. Make sure your spine is in neutral. Keep your arms by your sides, with the palms facing upward.

2 Lift your legs into the air, one at a time, at an angle of 90 degrees to your body.

3 Tighten your abdominal muscles and slowly lower one foot to the floor, then bring it back up again. Repeat this exercise using the other leg.

Toe touch

This exercise helps to flatten the deep transverse muscles.

1 Lie on your back on the floor with your spine in neutral, your knees over your hips, and your feet raised, parallel to the floor.

2 Tighten your abdominal muscles by gently pulling in your navel toward your backbone—do not suck in your waist or hold your breath.

3 Slowly lower one leg until your toes touch the floor. Move your leg back to the start position, then repeat on the other side.

Bin the broom handle

A long-practiced exercise is to place a pole or broom handle across your shoulders and, with your arms stretched along it, twist your body vigorously from side to side in the hope that this will help to whittle your waist. This sort of exercise actually does more harm than good because it produces a ballistic twisting movement around the spine (the axis of rotation). Not only are you likely to damage your obliques, but you may also stretch and tear tiny spinal ligaments. In addition, the weight of your upper body pressing down exerts extreme force on your spinal column—slipped disc, anyone? Ouch!

Cooling-down **exercises**

Just as you need to warm up the body for exercising, you also need to cool it down after you have finished. Try the two exercises shown on this spread, and take the time to cool down properly. Ideally, you should look to spend around ten minutes doing this.

Lying waist stretch

This is good for giving your body an all-over general stretch, and targets the obliques, the muscles at the side of your waist.

1 Lie on the floor on your back with your knees bent and your feet flat on the floor. Keep your arms stretched out to either side. Breathe in to prepare.

2 Breathe out and pull in your abdominal muscles. Slowly bend both knees to the left while turning your head to the right.

3 Hold for a count of ten, then return to the start position. Repeat, bending your knees to the other side.

Sitting body twister

You may find this stretch a little hard to perform, but this is a good way to mobilize your spine.

1 Sit on the floor with your legs straight out in front of you. Bend your right leg and cross it over your left knee.

2 Gently rotate your trunk and head toward your left as far as is comfortable, keeping your buttocks on the floor throughout.

3 Hold for a count of ten, then release and return to the start position. Repeat on the other side.

Legs and buttocks

If the hectic pace of daily life prevents your thighs, hips, and legs from getting the exercise they need to stay in tiptop shape, then this section is just what you need. It features quick, easy-to-follow exercise routines for toning and firming the bottom half of your body, all of which can be practiced in the comfort of your home!

Introduction

Unless you were born with a figure to rival that of a supermodel, you probably wish your lower half was slimmer and trimmer. The trouble is that hips and thighs are often hard to target—for example, the muscles in your legs are much bigger than those in your arms, so you need to put more effort into getting results.

The benefits

General exercise, such as running, isn't always effective, so the great thing about this section is that each and every one of the exercises focuses entirely on slimming down and toning up these trouble zones.

As you can imagine, most involve a lot of leg work and it may take some time for you to build up enough strength in the legs to be able to carry out the series of exercises outlined in the 12-week plan, but with practice it will get easier.

The muscles in the hips and thighs

It helps to have a basic understanding of the muscles you need to work on to exercise the bottom half of your body.

Buttocks: There are three buttock muscles—gluteus maximus (the biggest muscle in the body), medius, and minimus. They hold your pelvis in position, stabilize your hips, and balance the hip area.

Hamstrings: These are three long muscles below the buttock muscles, which run from the back of the hip bone to the back of the knees. The hamstrings work with the gluteus maximus to bend your knee and rotate your hips.

Hip flexors: A group of muscles that run from the hips to the spine and from various points along the thigh bone. They work in opposition to the buttock muscles, helping you to move your hips and lift your thighs and knees.

Quadriceps (quads): These are four muscles that run down the front of the thigh. They enable you to extend your legs and bend your hips.

Effective exercising

Tight quads and hamstrings cause poor posture and lower back pain so it's very important to keep them in good working order. If you only ever do one type of hip and thigh exercise, make it a squat, which really hits the spot!

Lunges are fantastic for firming your hips and thighs because they work the hip extensors, quadriceps, and hamstrings. They also improve your balance.

A helping hand for hips and thighs

For slimmer thighs and hips, follow a lowfat diet in addition to your toning and shaping routines:

- Trim all visible fat off meat.
- Steam or broil food rather than frying or boiling.
- Fill up with carbohydrates that release their energy slowly—for example, whole-grain pasta, rice, and cereals.
- Eat plenty of fresh fruit and vegetables.
- Drink plenty of water. This will flush out toxins from your body that can cause the appearance of dimpled flesh on your thighs.

As well as tightening up your gluteals, the bridging exercises will help to stabilize your pelvis and your trunk muscles, and work your hamstrings.

Do what you can!

Most of these muscle-building exercises are done as a series of repetitions. For exercises that need repeating in order to last for 30 seconds, simply do as many repetitions as you can comfortably achieve in that time.

What you'll need

For this section you will need a nonslip mat or pair of gym shoes, a chair, and a platform to step up on to or a sturdy bottom stair on a staircase.

Warming-up **exercises**

It is always essential to warm up before undertaking any form of exercise. Choose a couple of the exercises shown over the next few pages and spend a little time warming up. You should allow around ten minutes for this, and alternate them so you don't get bored.

2

Marching on the spot

This is a very easy and safe way to gently start warming up your body.

1 Stand with good posture, by having your feet hip-width distance apart, knees soft, stomach pulled in, and shoulders pulled back. Begin marching on the spot.

2 Be sure to keep your upper body straight and your stomach muscles pulled in. Aim to gradually lift your knees to hip height and then bend your arms and swing them back and forth as you would do if you were walking fast.

3 Do this for between two to three minutes until you feel fully warmed up. Alternatively, you can warm up by going for a brisk walk around the block.

Knee bends

This exercise loosens the hip-flexor muscles and helps to warm up all the leg muscles. Don't lock your knees as you do this, and bend only as far as is comfortable.

1 Stand with one hand resting on a support, such as a high-backed chair or a table, your feet hip-width apart, and slightly turned out. Tighten your abdominal muscles.

> **WATCH POINT**
> *Never point your toes inward while exercising— this can damage your knees.*

Exercise tip

Loosening up the body before exercising is important because it prepares the muscles and joints for the workout and also increases the heart rate, causing the blood to pump faster around the body. Consequently, the harder the muscles work, the more beneficial the exercise will be.

However, do not try to push any of the moves too far, too soon. Always keep the principles in mind and always think "quality."

2 Slowly bend your knees and lower your hips, then straighten up again. Use your buttock and leg muscles to lower and straighten.

3 Repeat ten times.

Standing knee lift

This exercise mobilizes the quadriceps and the hip flexors at the front of your body.

1 Stand up straight with your left hand on a chair to balance you.

2 Tighten your abdominal muscles.

3 Pull up your right knee so that your foot is parallel to your left knee.

4 Release and repeat on the other leg.

3

Standing leg circles

This exercise warms up the buttock muscles by lifting and drawing them together.

1 Stand up straight with good posture, with your knees soft, and legs hip-width apart. For balance, hold on to a chair.

2 Tighten your abdominal muscles by gently pulling in your navel toward your backbone.

3 Lift your left leg a few inches off the floor and gently circle it one way, then the other.

4 Return to the start position and repeat on the other leg.

Exercise tip

Be sure to use a straight-backed, sturdy chair when exercising—not one on castors.

3

Introductory **exercises**

These first-stage exercises are aimed at beginners so you should find them relatively easy to start with, allowing you to become more involved as you progress. If you find any of the exercises a little too difficult, simply replace them with something else of the same level.

Basic squat

Targeting the buttocks and tops of the thighs, this easy exercise is great for toning up those trouble spots.

1 Stand up with good posture, your feet hip-width apart, and your hands on your hips.

2 Tighten your abdominal muscles by gently pulling your navel toward your spine.

3 Bend your knees and squat as if you were going to sit down. Only squat as far as is comfortable.

Exercise tip

If you only ever do one type of hip and thigh exercise, make it a squat, which really hits the spot! Squats work the hip extensors, hamstrings (back of thigh muscles), and quadriceps (front of thigh muscles).

4 Return to the standing position by pushing through your heels, keeping your knees slightly bent as you do so.

3

Standing calf raises

The calf muscles are hard to target, although studies have shown that walking in high heels can help to tone them up! To get really sexy, shapely calves, we recommend you try this exercise instead.

1 Stand with both feet near the edge of a raised object, such as a stair or a big chunky book. Place the ball of your right foot on the edge of the raised object, letting your heel extend off the edge.

2 Hold on to a wall or a chair for support and, lifting your left leg into the air slightly by bending at the knee, gently let your right heel drop down until you feel the stretch in your calf. Keep your back straight, your head up, and your right leg straight.

3 Rise up on to your right toe as high as you can and hold for a second while flexing the calf muscle.

4 Carefully return to the start position, then repeat with the left leg.

> **WATCH POINT**
> *Make sure that you don't slip off the raised object by carefully controlling the move. If that means you have to do fewer than ten reps on each foot during the exercise, so be it.*

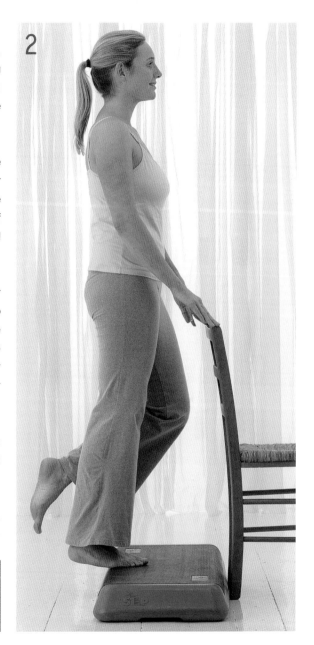

Bridge squeeze

This buttock-clenching exercise makes the gluteus maximus work to support your back. If you feel a strong contraction in your hamstrings or any strain in your lower back, then you are not using your buttock muscles properly.

Exercise tip

As well as tightening up your gluteals, this bridging exercise will help to stabilize your pelvis and your trunk muscles, and work your hamstrings. Take care not to overarch your back or let it sag, and remember to keep your breathing steady and controlled throughout.

1 Lie on your back with your knees bent and feet slightly apart.

2 Tighten your abdominal muscles by gently drawing in your navel toward your spine—which will protect your back muscles.

3 Curl your bottom off the floor, lifting your pelvis until your knees, hips, and chest are in line.

4 Hold this for a count of ten, squeezing your buttock muscles to support the bridge position. Release and repeat.

3

Superman

You need to have a good sense of balance to do this exercise, so if you don't get it right first time, be patient. It's great for increasing stability and endurance in the joints, as well as working the core muscles in your thighs.

1 Get down on the floor on all fours, then pull in your abdominal muscles.

2 Extend your right arm out in front of you and your left leg out behind you, keeping them as straight as you can without locking your elbow or knee. Engage your abdominal muscles to help prevent your back from arching—it will reduce any risk of injury. You will feel the muscles working in the thigh of your extended leg. If you want to increase the effects, point your toes—it will make you tense your muscles even harder. Keep your head and neck in line with your back to make sure that you're not twisting your neck.

3 Slowly return to the start position and repeat with the opposite leg and arm.

Inner thigh lift

These side-lying exercises work your inner thigh muscles (abductors). Remember to keep your spine in neutral and your stomach muscles tightened throughout.

1 Lie on one side with your hips facing forward and your body in a straight line. Prop yourself up on your elbow, with your head resting on your hand, and place the other hand on the floor in front of you for support.

2 Tighten your stomach muscles by gently drawing in your navel toward your spine to protect your back.

3 Bend your top leg so that the knee touches the floor in front of you.

4 Raise the bottom extended leg, keeping the knee soft (slightly bent), then lower.

5 Do all of your repetitions on one side, then repeat them on the other side of your body.

Outer thigh lift

Make sure that you perform each move slowly and in a controlled way, to really work the muscles. You don't have to tense your buttocks as you do this, but it's good to work your gluteals whenever you can.

1 Lie on your right side with your body in a straight line and your thighs and feet together. Prop yourself up with your right arm and rest your left hand on the floor in front of you. Tighten your stomach muscles by drawing your navel in toward your spine—this will help to protect your back.

2 Bend both knees. Lift up the top leg, then lower, squeezing your buttocks together as you raise and lower your leg.

3 Do all your repetitions on one side, then repeat on the other side of your body.

Keeping up your motivation

All too often, people start a new exercise regime burning with enthusiasm, only for it to peter out very quickly to the point where they can't be bothered to do anything at all. When you start your exercise program, be realistic about how and when you can do it. You need to set aside a regular slot for your routine so it becomes a natural and automatic part of your everyday routine. But if you do miss several days, don't get disheartened and quit—a little exercise, even on a very irregular basis, is still better than nothing at all.

WATCH POINT
Keep the knee of the extended leg soft (slightly bent).

Advanced **exercises**

Now that you've worked through the introductory exercises and are feeling fitter and more confident, you can progress to this second series of exercises. As before, if you find any particular exercises difficult, simply replace them with something else from this level.

Lunge

The further you step forward in this exercise, the harder your muscles will be worked.

1 Stand with your hands on your hips and your feet parallel and hip-width apart. Brace your abdominal muscles.

2 Take a big step forward, keeping your weight evenly balanced between both legs.

3 Bend both knees as far as is comfortable so that you lower your torso down, then return to the start position.

4 Repeat on the other leg.

1

3

Double knee bends

This exercise, which strengthens your thighs, calves, and buttocks, will help you to achieve the sculpted legs of a dancer.

1 Stand with your legs a little wider than shoulder-width apart and your feet slightly turned out. Rest your hands on the back of a chair to help you to balance.

2 Tighten your abdominal muscles to protect your lower back.

3 Slowly press your knees out and lower yourself down. You should feel this in your buttocks and the back of your thighs.

4 Return to standing, then tense your buttocks, squeeze your inner thigh muscles, and rise up on to your toes. Return to the start position.

One-legged buttock clencher

This is a harder exercise that will really work your gluteals.

1 Lie on your back with your knees bent and your feet flat on the floor, slightly apart. Keep your arms by your sides, palms facing downward.

2 Place your left foot on to your right knee. Tighten your abdominal muscles to support your back.

3 Press your lower back down into the floor and gently tilt your pelvis forward, so that the pubic bone rises. Lift your hips off the floor and squeeze your buttock muscles, then release.

4 Do all your repetitions on one leg, then repeat on the other leg.

Bridge with leg lift

Lifting one leg strengthens the muscles at the back of the buttocks and thighs, while increasing balance and control in your stabilizing muscles.

1 Lie on your back with your knees bent and feet slightly apart, and your arms at your sides.

2 Tighten your abdominal muscles by gently drawing in your navel toward your spine.

3 Curl your bottom off the floor, lifting your pelvis until your knees, hips, and chest are in line.

Controlling your movements

Make sure that all exercises are performed slowly, carefully, and with your full attention. You really do need to concentrate on what you're doing and think about how your body is responding to any exercise.

If an action hurts or you do it too quickly, then you're not doing it properly. Movements should flow in a gentle, controlled manner. This enables your muscles to stretch naturally.

4 Extend one leg, lift it level with the knee, then lower to the floor. Do all your repetitions on one leg, then repeat on the other leg.

4

Cooling-down **exercises**

Just as you need to warm up the body for exercising, you also need to cool it down after you have finished. Try the two exercises shown on this spread, and take the time to cool down properly. Ideally, you should look to spend around ten minutes doing this.

2

Standing quad stretch

Depending on how flexible you are, this stretch may feel quite hard to do at first, but it quickly becomes easier.

1 Stand up straight with your feet hip-width apart and your knees soft (slightly bent). Tighten your stomach muscles to protect your back.

2 Bend your left leg up behind you and hold your foot or ankle with your left hand.

3 Hold for 20 seconds, then release and repeat on the other side.

4 Repeat twice more on each leg.

Lying hamstring stretch

If you don't stretch, tight hamstrings can cause the hips and pelvis to rotate backward, resulting in bad posture.

1 Lie on your back with your knees bent and your feet resting flat on the floor.

2 Lift one leg and grasp the back of the thigh with your hands.

3 Gently pull that leg toward your chest as far as is comfortable. Repeat on the other leg.

Top tips for stretching

- Only stretch warm muscles.
- Slowly ease the muscles into position.
- Never bounce into position.
- Do not overstretch—mild discomfort is acceptable, but if it hurts you should stop.
- Breathe freely to enable blood to flow to the muscles—do not hold your breath.

Start marching!

Before you begin your stretches, it is a good idea to march on the spot for a couple of minutes to gently bring your heart rate and body temperature back to their pre-exercise state. Do this by gradually easing your march to a slow pace and then coming to a halt.

3

Core
stability

Core stability is the effective use of the core muscles to help stabilize the spine, allowing your limbs to move more freely. The positive effects of good core stability include reducing the likelihood of injury, better posture, increased agility and flexibility, and improved coordination.

Introduction

Core training is a workout that strengthens your body from the inside out by concentrating on the muscles that form your "core." The core of your body is simply what's between the shoulders and hips—basically, the trunk and pelvis. Core training re-educates these muscles to make them more effective.

The core is a crucial group of muscles, not only for sports, but for normal daily activities as well, because it comes into play just about every time you move. This is why it is so important that your core is strong. Once you have learned how to strengthen your core, your lower abdominal muscles will be drawn in toward the spine and help you sit up straight. Your balance and coordination will be improved and, most important of all, the stability these muscles bring will help keep your spine healthy and flexible.

What is core stability?

Core stability is the effective use of the core muscles to help stabilize the spine, allowing your limbs to move more freely. Good core stability means that you can keep your midsection rigid without forces, such as gravity, affecting your movements. The positive effects of this include reducing the chance of injury, better posture, increased agility and flexibility, and improved coordination.

Core stability can be increased by developing trunk fitness, which is necessary for everyday life, not just for sports. To really capture the benefits of core strength, it is necessary to work the deep, underlying abdominal and back musculature.

Equipment

The amount of equipment you need is up to you—there are plenty of pieces of equipment that create an unstable base and make your core muscles work really hard. For the purpose of this chapter we recommend using an exercise ball for variation, but if you don't want to buy one, there are plenty of exercises to choose from to begin with. An exercise mat is also recommended, and small cushions or folded towels make ideal padding during exercises that involve lying on the floor, or kneeling.

Core muscles

The muscles you need to know about for improving your core stability are those that are arranged around your torso, or trunk.

The trunk muscles fall into two categories: inner (mainly responsible for stabilization) and outer (mainly responsible for movement). The inner unit muscles include the transversus abdominis, diaphragm, multifidous, and pelvic floor; the outer unit includes the obliques and spinal erectors. The inner and outer units work together to create spinal stability and enable subsequent movement.

How to train your core

The core muscles should be loaded with resistance, and challenged in a variety of ways—by lateral (side) flexion, bending forward and backward, and rotation. If strength and muscle development are the goals, hundreds of repetitions are not necessary. Core strength should be developed gradually, to decrease the risk of injury. When starting out on a core-training program, you need to progress properly:

- Start with the easiest movements and progress to more difficult movements.
- Perform all movements in a slow and controlled manner until coordination, strength, and confidence permit higher-speed ones.
- To increase the complexity and muscle demands of the exercises, many moves can be performed lying prone (face down) or supine (on your back), on an exercise ball or other unstable platform, after you have mastered them on the floor.

Warming-up **exercises**

It is always essential to warm up before undertaking any form of exercise. Choose a couple of the exercises shown over the next few pages and spend a little time warming up. You should allow around ten minutes for this, and alternate them so you don't get bored.

2

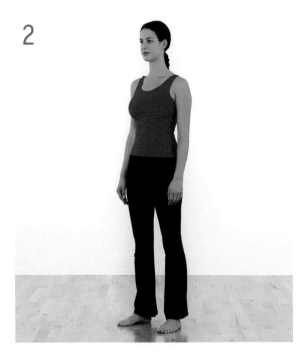

Standing abdominal hollowing

For all the core-stability exercises you have to activate the deep, inner-unit muscles in a hollowing action, so this exercise is an essential part of your warm-up.

1 Stand tall with your feet hip-width apart and your spine in neutral.

2 Pull your stomach muscles in and up to hollow your abdomen, keeping your attention focused on your navel. Imagine that there is a belt around your waist and that you are simply tightening the belt by one notch. Hold for a count of five.

3 Perform three repetitions.

WATCH POINT
The action should feel light and subtle—do not hold your breath or suck in your waist because you won't be using your deep stabilizing muscles. Keep your hips, legs, and spine still and restrict movement to your stomach muscles alone—try not to flatten your back.

Core stability

Torso rotations

Gradually, increase the range of movement as you do this exercise, reaching across your torso with your opposite hand as you do so. The twisting action should force you to come up on to the toes of your opposite foot.

1 Keep your pelvis in neutral and stand with your feet hip-width apart and knees slightly bent.

2 Rotate your torso to one side, then the other, increasing the range of movement as you do so. You should feel a slight stretch across your back and shoulders.

3 Perform five to ten turning press repetitions.

2

> **WATCH POINT**
> *Always work slowly and with control, and do not push your body further than it naturally goes—you should not feel any pain or discomfort when doing these exercises. Over time, you will become more flexible and will naturally be able to stretch further.*

Introductory **exercises**

These first-stage exercises are aimed at beginners, so you should find them relatively easy to start with, allowing you to become more involved as you progress. If you find any of the exercises a little too difficult, simply replace them with something else of the same level.

1

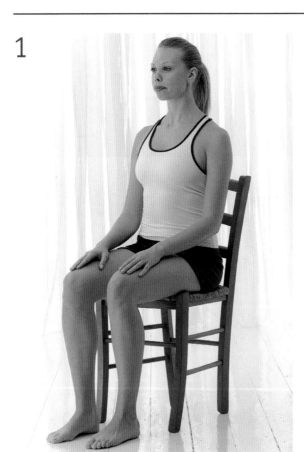

Seated stomach workout

This tones and flattens your deep stomach muscle (transversus abdominis) and the one that runs down the front of your stomach (the rectus abdominis).

1 Sit forward on a chair. Keep your feet flat on the floor, hip-width apart, with your knees over your ankles, and your palms on your thighs.

2 Sit up straight. Tighten the abdominal muscles by gently pulling your navel in toward your spine. Hold for ten seconds, then relax.

3 Rest for a count of three before doing any repetitions.

WATCH POINT
Breathe regularly as you do this exercise—don't hold your breath because it will make your blood pressure rise, which can be dangerous when exercising.

114

Squat with leg lift

This move works your entire lower body. Focus on keeping your abdominal muscles braced to maintain your balance.

1 Stand on the floor with your feet parallel and hip-width apart. Place your hands on your hips, set your abdominal muscles, and bend your knees so that you squat down.

2 Press up into a standing position, as you simultaneously extend your right leg to the side.

3 Return to the squatting position.

4 Repeat on the other side.

2

Seated reverse abdominal curl

This is an easy exercise that can be done almost anywhere. It works your rectus abdominis. Try to avoid sagging or arching the back and hold your abdominal muscles in tight throughout the movement.

1 Sit on a stool or a bench with good posture. Set your abdominal muscles and extend your arms in front of you at shoulder height.

2 Slowly lean your torso and shoulders backward, keeping the spine rigid, as far back as is comfortable.

3 Hold the position for a count of two, then return to the start position.

1

2

Waist twist

Make sure that you have a lot of space around you so that when you swing your arms you don't hit anything. This is a fun exercise to do and it really gets to work on the obliques (the muscles at the side of your waist), to help define a curvy silhouette.

1 Stand with your feet hip-width apart, hands by your sides and knees slightly bent.

2 Extend your arms out in front of you and form loose fists with both hands.

3 Swing your arms from side to side, making sure that your feet stay firmly on the floor, and that your hips face forward. Start off slowly and then build up speed, making sure you keep control of the movement and that your hips stay facing the front.

4 When approximately 30 seconds have passed, drop your arms back down by your sides and return to the start position.

> **WATCH POINT**
> *Don't get carried away while swinging your arms as you may end up pulling a muscle. If you have to go slowly to control the movement, so be it.*

3

Introductory **exercises**

Here is your starter six-week plan. We recommend that you begin with and follow the introductory exercises before embarking on the advanced sessions. Make sure that each day you warm up before the exercise routine and, at the end, allow time to cool down and stretch. To start, aim to do one or two sets of ten repetitions for each exercise. Don't feel that you have to complete the whole routine—you can build up the amount of repetitions (reps) as you progress.

Week **1**

One or two sets of ten reps

Day 1 Chest and back

Easy plank p34
C-curve p35
Standing wall press-up p36
Bust lift p37
Bell pull p38

Day 2 Arms and shoulders

Biceps curl p54
Triceps squeeze back p55
Front raises p56
Front arm toner (hammer
   curl) p57

Day 3 Stomach

Belly tightener p74
Side reach p75
Spine rotation p76
Reverse curl p77

Day 4 Legs and buttocks

Basic squat p94
Standing calf raises p95
Bridge squeeze p96

Day 5 Core stability

Seated stomach workout p114
Squat with leg lift p115
Seated reverse abdominal
   curl p116
Waist twist p117

Day 6 Legs and buttocks

Superman p97
Inner thigh lift p98
Outer thigh lift p99

Day 7 Mixed combination

Easy plank p34
Standing wall press-up p36
Biceps curl p54
Basic squat p94
Seated reverse abdominal
   curl p116

Week 2

One or two sets of ten reps

Day 1 Stomach
Belly tightener p74
Side reach p75
Spine rotation p76
Reverse curl p77

Day 2 Chest and back
Bust lift p37
Bell pull p38
Criss-cross arms p39

Day 3 Legs and buttocks
Bridge squeeze p96
Superman p97
Inner thigh lift p98
Outer thigh lift p99

Day 4 Stomach
Spine rotation p76
Reverse curl p77
Leg slide p78
Abdominal curl p79

Day 5 Arms and shoulders
Biceps curl p54
Triceps squeeze back p55
Superwoman arms p58
Kneeling boxed press-up p59

Day 6 Core stability
Waist twist p117
Single leg stretch p118
Side leg lift p119

Day 7 Mixed combination
Kneeling boxed press-up p59
Abdominal curl p79
Basic squat p94
Bridge squeeze p96

Reps—weeks 1–3
One repetition equals one exercise, following the step-by-step instructions. A set is a group of repetitions and at this point of the program we advise that you complete one to two sets of ten repetitions for each exercise.

Keeping up your motivation
When you first start your program, be realistic about how and when you can do it. You do need to set aside a regular slot for your routine so it becomes a natural and automatic part of your everyday life, just like brushing your teeth. But if you do miss several days, don't get disheartened and quit—a little exercise even on a very irregular basis is still better than nothing at all!

Acknowledgments

Photography credits: Ian Parsons, all exercise pictures;
iStockphoto 8 (both images), 9, 10, 13 (top right), 18, 20, 22, 23, 24, 25
Cover image: Dumbbell and exercise mat © Comstock Images/Getty Images